So Many Sounds

**Written by
Dana Meachen Rau**

**Illustrated by
Kristin Sorra**

SCHOLASTIC INC.

New York   Toronto   London   Auckland   Sydney
Mexico City   New Delhi   Hong Kong   Buenos Aires

For Kelly, a good listener
—D. M. R.

For Dennis
—K. S.

Reading Consultant
Katharine A. Kane
Education Consultant
(Retired, San Diego County Office of Education
and San Diego State University)

ISBN 0-516-23845-0

12 11 10 9 8 7 6 5 4 3   1 2 3 4 5 6/0

Printed in the U.S.A.   10

First Scholastic printing, September 2001

So many sounds
to listen to.

Listen to the bird.

Coo. Coo.

Listen to the cow.

Moo. Moo.

Listen to the farmer.

Shoo! Shoo!

Listen to the train.

Choo. Choo.

Listen to the owl.

Hoo. Hoo.

Word List (16 words)

bird	listen	sounds
choo	many	the
coo	moo	to
cow	owl	train
farmer	shoo	
hoo	so	

About the Author

Dana Meachen Rau is the author of many books for children, including historical fiction, storybooks, biographies, and numerous books in the Rookie Reader series. She also works as an illustrator and editor. When she's not busily typing on her computer or buried in piles of paper, she listens to sounds with her husband, Chris, and son, Charlie, in Farmington, Connecticut.

About the Illustrator

Kristin Sorra was born and raised in Baltimore, Maryland. She always loved to draw and paint, so she pursued her love of art at Pratt Institute in Brooklyn, New York, where she studied illustration. She even married a fellow illustrator and now lives in Garnerville, New York.